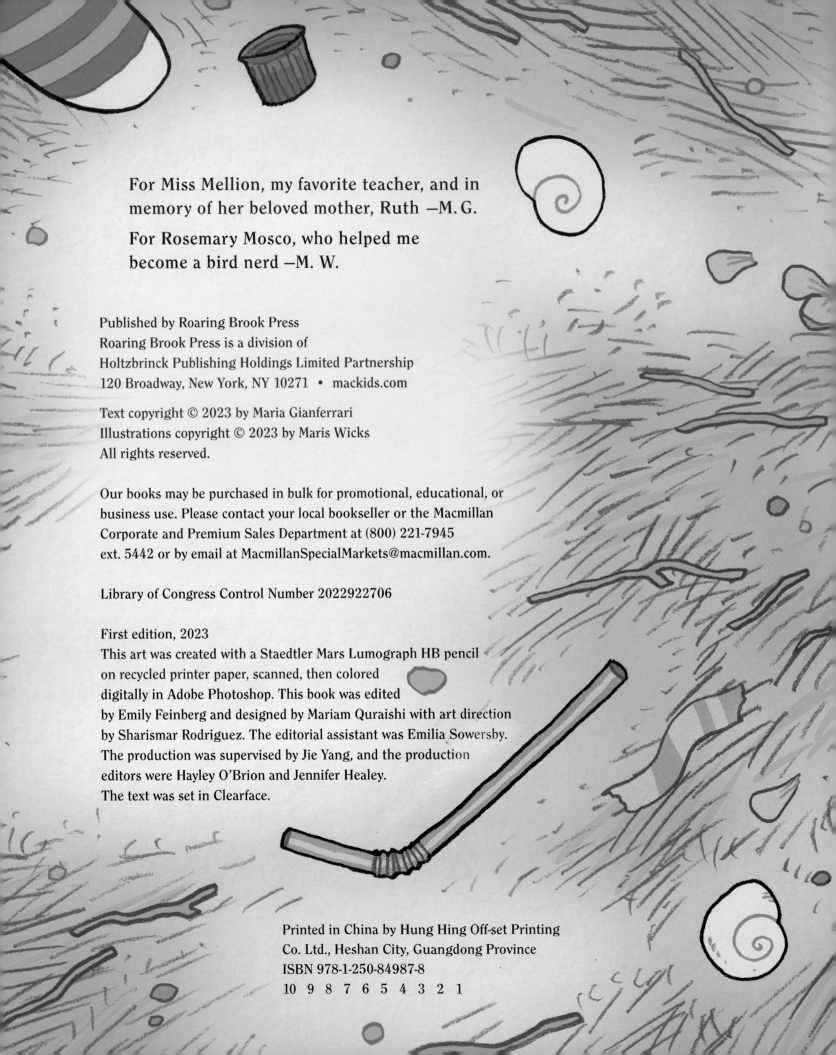

For Miss Mellion, my favorite teacher, and in memory of her beloved mother, Ruth —M. G.

For Rosemary Mosco, who helped me become a bird nerd —M. W.

Published by Roaring Brook Press
Roaring Brook Press is a division of
Holtzbrinck Publishing Holdings Limited Partnership
120 Broadway, New York, NY 10271 • mackids.com

Our books may be purchased in bulk for promotional, educational, or business use. Please contact your local bookseller or the Macmillan Corporate and Premium Sales Department at (800) 221-7945 ext. 5442 or by email at MacmillanSpecialMarkets@macmillan.com.

Library of Congress Control Number 2022922706

First edition, 2023
This art was created with a Staedtler Mars Lumograph HB pencil on recycled printer paper, scanned, then colored digitally in Adobe Photoshop. This book was edited by Emily Feinberg and designed by Mariam Quraishi with art direction by Sharismar Rodriguez. The editorial assistant was Emilia Sowersby. The production was supervised by Jie Yang, and the production editors were Hayley O'Brion and Jennifer Healey. The text was set in Clearface.

Printed in China by Hung Hing Off-set Printing Co. Ltd., Heshan City, Guangdong Province
ISBN 978-1-250-84987-8
10 9 8 7 6 5 4 3 2 1

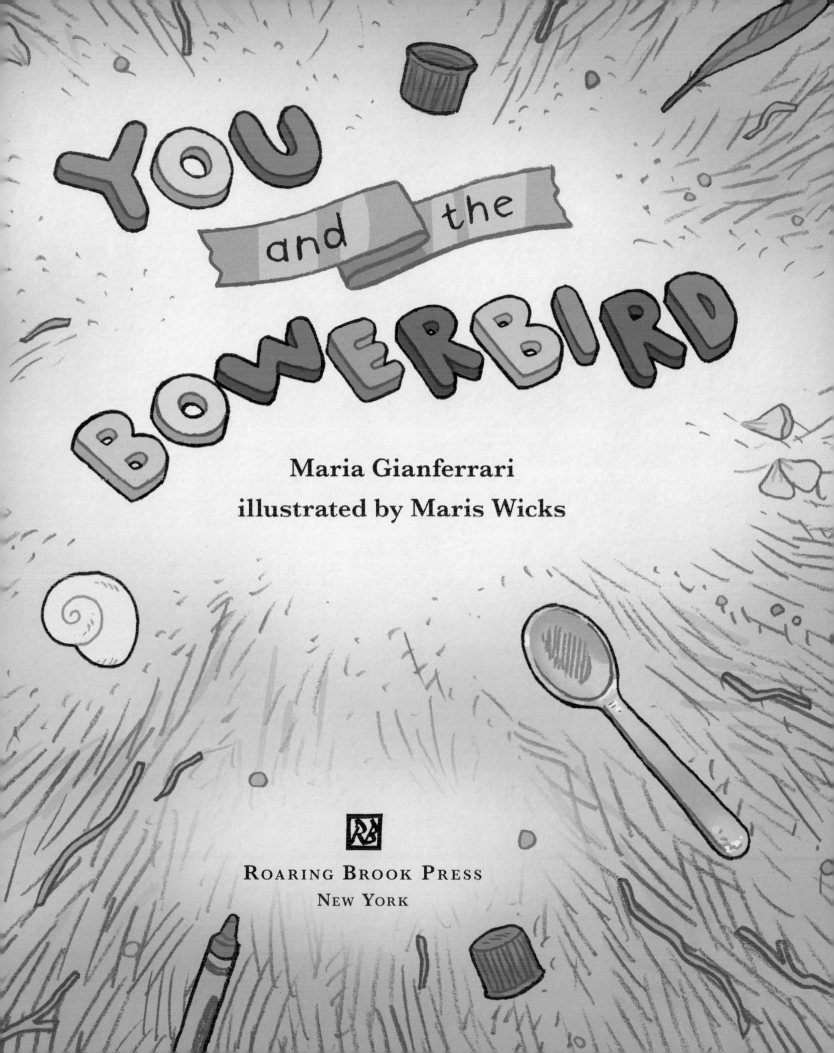

YOU and the BOWERBIRD

Maria Gianferrari

illustrated by Maris Wicks

ROARING BROOK PRESS

NEW YORK

Have you seen the
blue-black bird?

On the edge of the rain forest,
you watch.

His eyes are lilac marbles.
His curved beak,
so much like the sun.

It's a satin bowerbird.

Satin collects twigs,

shaping

spreading

making.

Wings sprout
from the ground.

It's time to decorate his bower.
Satin nibbles pine needles . . .

Satin gathers azure treasures
as pleasing as his feathers:

TREE HOUSE

oops I left my marbles out!

clothespins and bottle caps,

BERRIES

. . . to paint his walls.

FLOWERS

BINS

HOUSE

trash

spoons and straws,

BOTTLE
CAP

ROCKS

marbles and yarn.

A rosella parrot feather waits
like a welcome mat.

Still, something is missing . . .

Other bowerbirds inspect.

In flies a female,
pea-soup green,
lilac eyes shining.

Pea peeks and pecks.

Pirate steals away,
feather in his beak.

When Satin returns, he scours his bower.

Where is his welcome mat?

Blue socks wave
like flags in the wind.

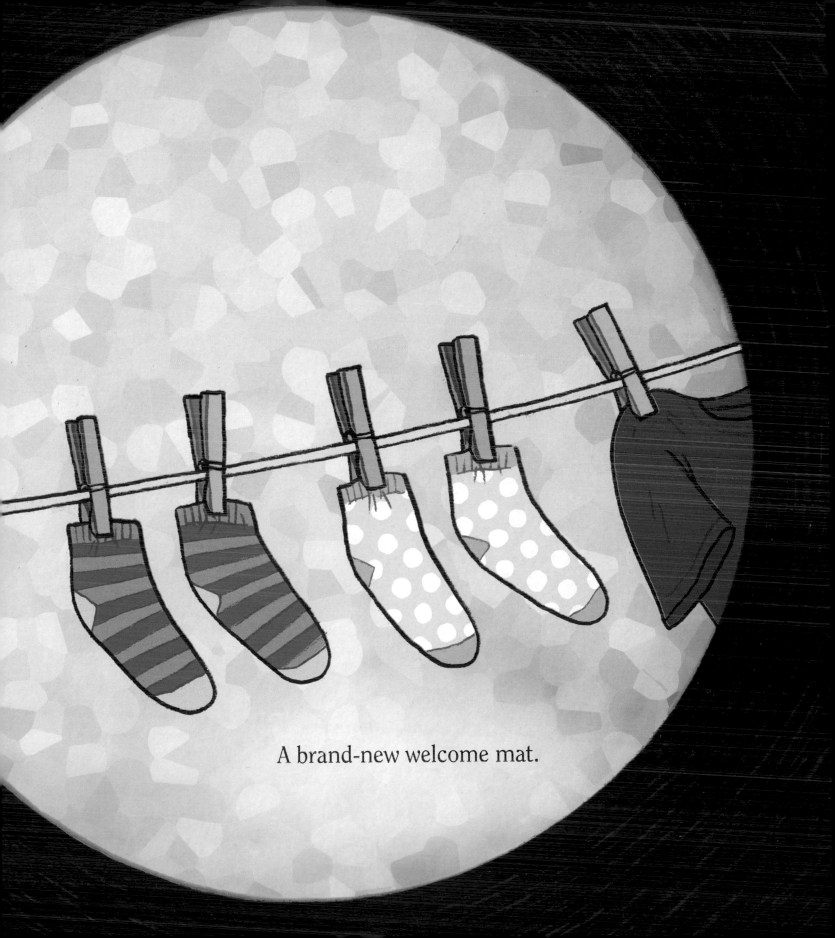

A brand-new welcome mat.

Pea skips and creeps, lilac eyes shining.

Pirate snatches Satin's sock.

Satin's welcome mat is gone.

Again.

Will he find another?

While Satin's away,
juniors loot!

Pirate pillages,
too.

Satin inspects:

Twisted twigs.

Shredded flowers.

Stolen straws.

So much is missing—
and he still needs a welcome mat.

You help.

Satin patches

and places.

The bower
is ready.

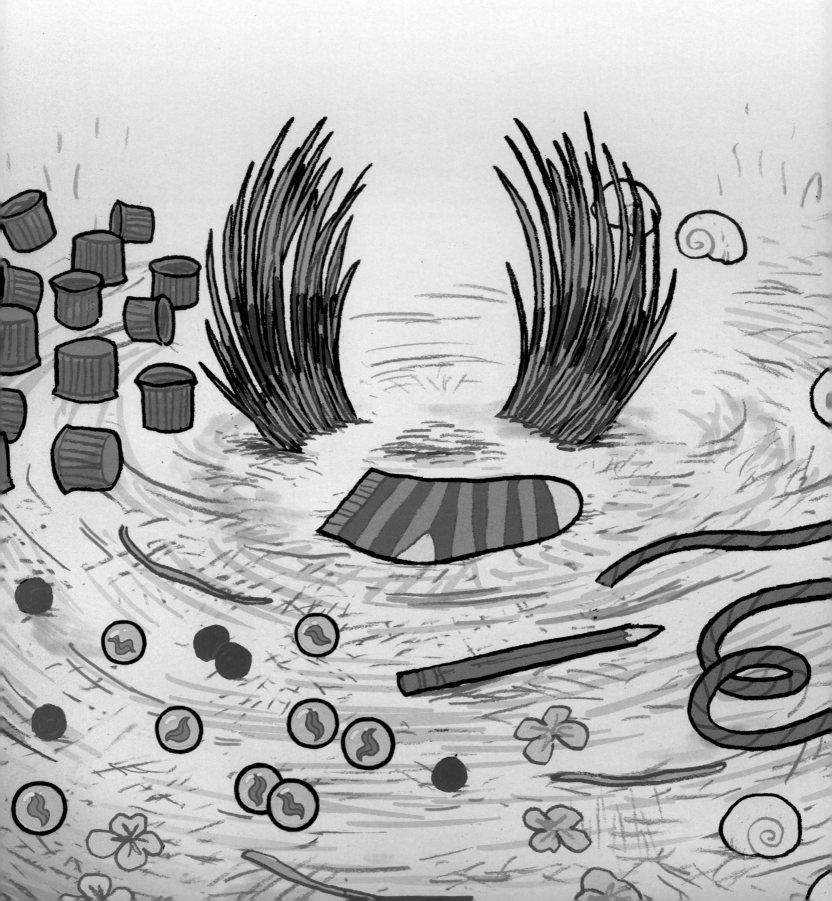

Satin's welcome mat still waits.

A song and dance for Pea.

Lilac eyes flash in the sun.

Inside the rain forest,
Pea sculpts her nest—
lillypilly lined,
cradled in mistletoe—
and lays her eggs.

Before long, nestlings become

fledglings, full bloom.

Peep
Peep
Peep

And, in time, adults in search of mates.

In search of blue.

You—

Line up letters.

Group crayons.

Place marbles.

On the edge of the rain forest . . .

. . . bowerbirds are coming.

BOWER POWER

HAVE YOU SEEN THE SATIN BOWERBIRD?

G'day, mate! Welcome to Oz, otherwise known as Australia, home of the satin bowerbird. Satin bowerbirds live in eastern and southeastern Australia. There are twenty species of bowerbirds.

MAKING & PAINTING THEIR BACHELOR PADS

Male satin bowerbirds build their avenue bowers, U-shaped structures with thousands of sticks, along edge habitats near rain forests and woodlands. They also "paint" their inside walls using a mixture of saliva and chewed-up pine needles. But their bowers aren't nests—they're more like decked-out bachelor pads designed to attract female mates.

BLUE HUES & BOWER ADORNMENTS

Satin bowerbirds are known for their decorative, blue-hued bowers. They collect an assortment of blue artificial objects, many of them plastic, as adornments: buttons, bottle caps, clothespins, ribbons, yarn, marbles, glass bits, and more. Watch out! They might steal your favorite socks from the clothesline! Some scientists think bowerbirds seek out these blue objects because they complement the birds' shiny plumage, while others believe the objects are prized since they're scarce in nature. Satin bowerbirds also decorate their bowers with objects from the natural world such as flowers, sloughed snake skins, snail shells, feathers, and insects.

PIRATES & PILLAGERS

It's a break in! When a male bowerbird is away from his bower, rival males both mature and juvenile sneak in and mess it up. They also steal their rivals' prized treasures for their own bowers. The most coveted objects, rosella parrot feathers and bottle caps, get stolen and passed from bower to bower. Juvenile males resemble females in their green coloring and don't get their dark satin plumage until around age seven, when it's time to attract a mate.

FEMALE BOWERBIRDS

Females first tour the bower site while the males are away. She may peck on the paint, and if she likes what she sees, she visits the bower a second time when the male is present. During this pre-nest-building phase of mate selection, a female may visit several different bower sites. Male bower owners court a visiting female by running in front of the bower and inviting her to join in, usually holding a decoration in his beak. Males fluff their feathers, open and fold their wings, and lift and lower their tails while making whirring and buzzing courtship calls. Females retreat inside the forest to begin building their nests. Once finished, females return to their favorite bowers and choose a single mate.

DECORATOR OR DANCER?

Some scientists believe that young females choose a mate based on how much she likes his decorations, especially if they're blue. An older female, on the other hand, may be more interested in the male's dance moves. But the most successful male satin bowerbirds are multitalented, acting as architects and interior decorators as well as singers and dancers.

BOWERBIRD NESTS, NESTLINGS & FLEDGLINGS

Females build their nests in trees, vines, or clumps of mistletoe. They line their nests with eucalyptus, acacia, lillypilly, and other leaves and lay a clutch averaging two eggs. Nestlings eat fruit and insects such as beetles, cicadas, and grasshoppers. They fledge (leave the nest) after approximately three weeks. Adult females begin their search for mates in their second and third years. Males are not fully mature until around age seven.

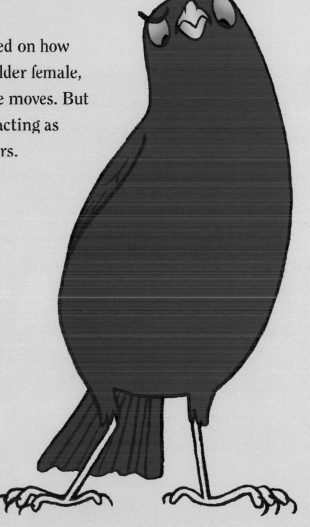

To learn more about satin bowerbirds, explore these resources:
- *Birds of a Feather: Bowerbirds and Me* by Susan L. Roth
- Animalia, animalia.bio/satin-bowerbird
- BBC Earth, "Odd Bird Seduction Techniques," youtu.be/_H9TyXiXM2k
- Cornell Lab of Ornithology's eBird, ebird.org/species/satbow1
- "Satin Bowerbird Courtship Behavior," youtu.be/1EN9k6LEulg
- "Satin Bowerbird Sounds & Calls," wildambience.com/wildlife-sounds/satin-bowerbird/

To learn more about all kinds of bowerbirds, visit:
- Sir David Attenborough's "Bowerbirds: The Art of Seduction" at BBC Natural World 2000, dailymotion.com/video/x63qoip
- The San Diego Zoo, animals.sandiegozoo.org/animals/bowerbird